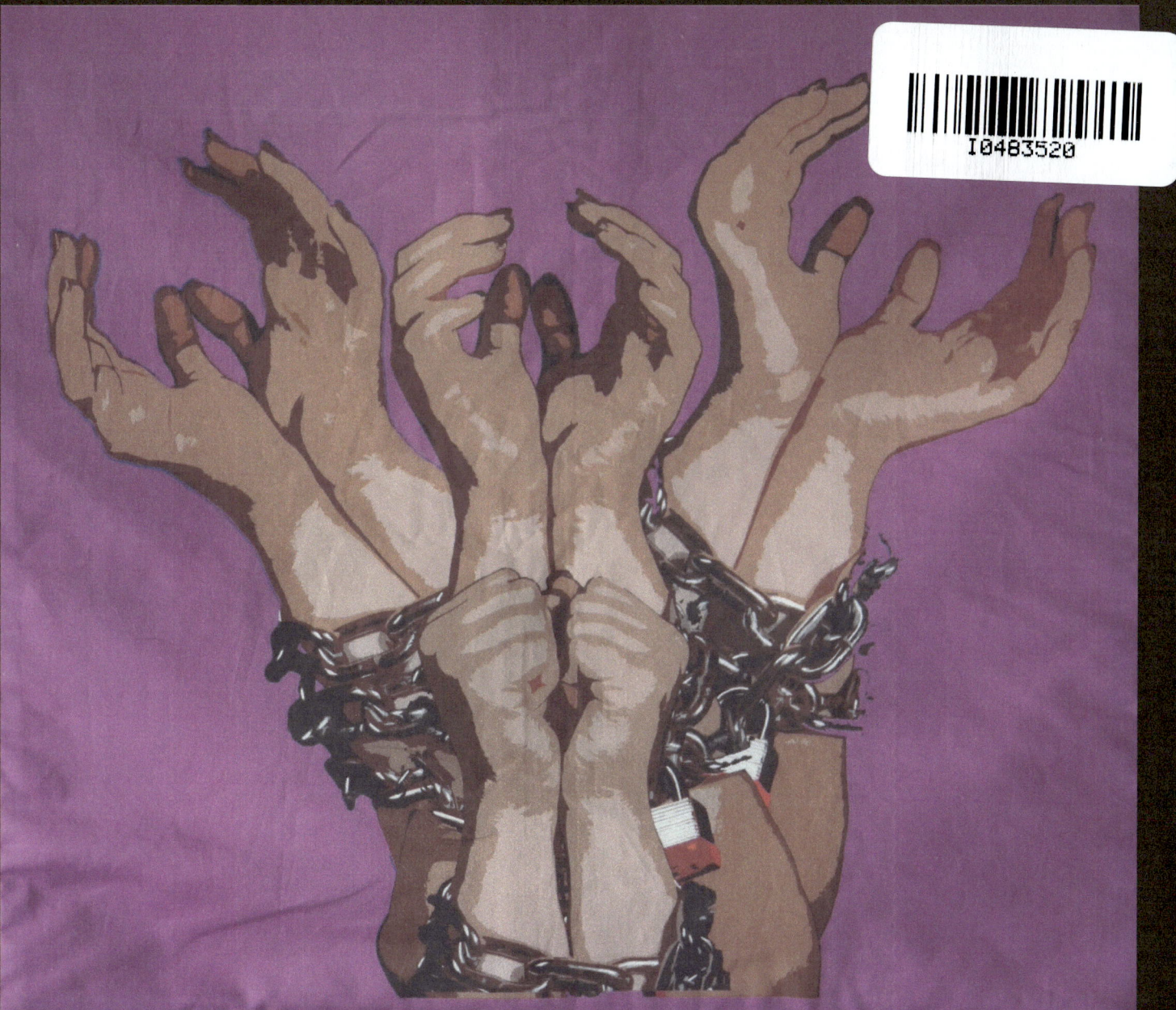

UNMADE BED

Debra Calkins, Artist

Michael Stadler, Photographer

IN GRATITUDE

Fiber 19 – who were there from the very beginning and through all my trials

Michael Stadler – photographer extraordinaire

Stephanie Patrick – for the music for this installation; everything I wished for

Louise Roby – PDF queen

Larkin Jean Van Horn – for the Heart Labyrinth, listening and making suggestions

Anne Davenport – for listening and making suggestions

Rachel, 14 year old model

ARTIST STATEMENT

The average age of the young woman on the street
is fourteen. The men who control her tell her she is
worthless even as they sell her thirty to one
hundred times a day.

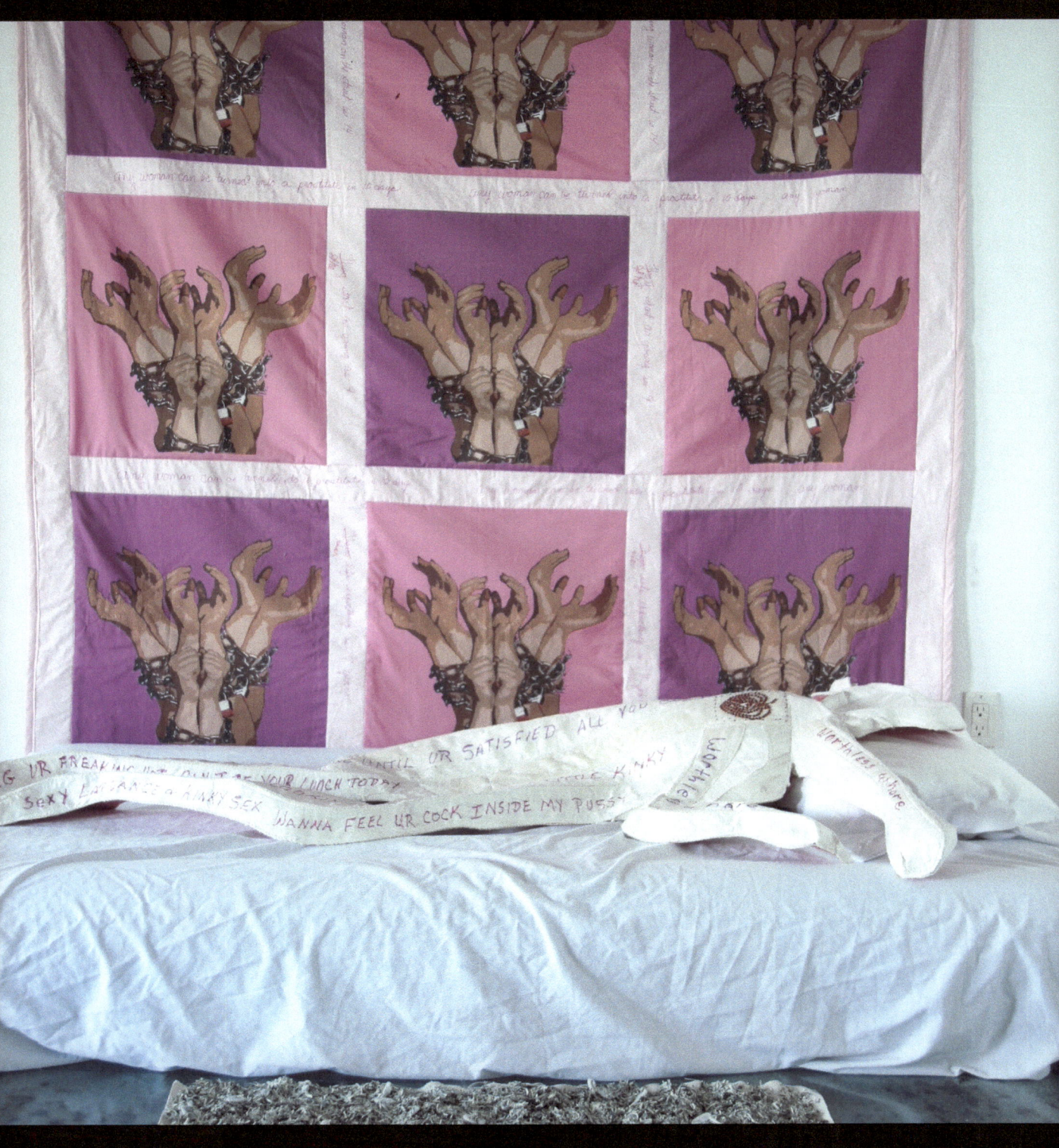

They keep her in line with violence, physical pain, abuse, drugs, and alcohol. On average, she will die in seven years. If you are a woman and think it will never happen to you, think again. Pimps brag that any woman can be turned into a prostitute in ten days.

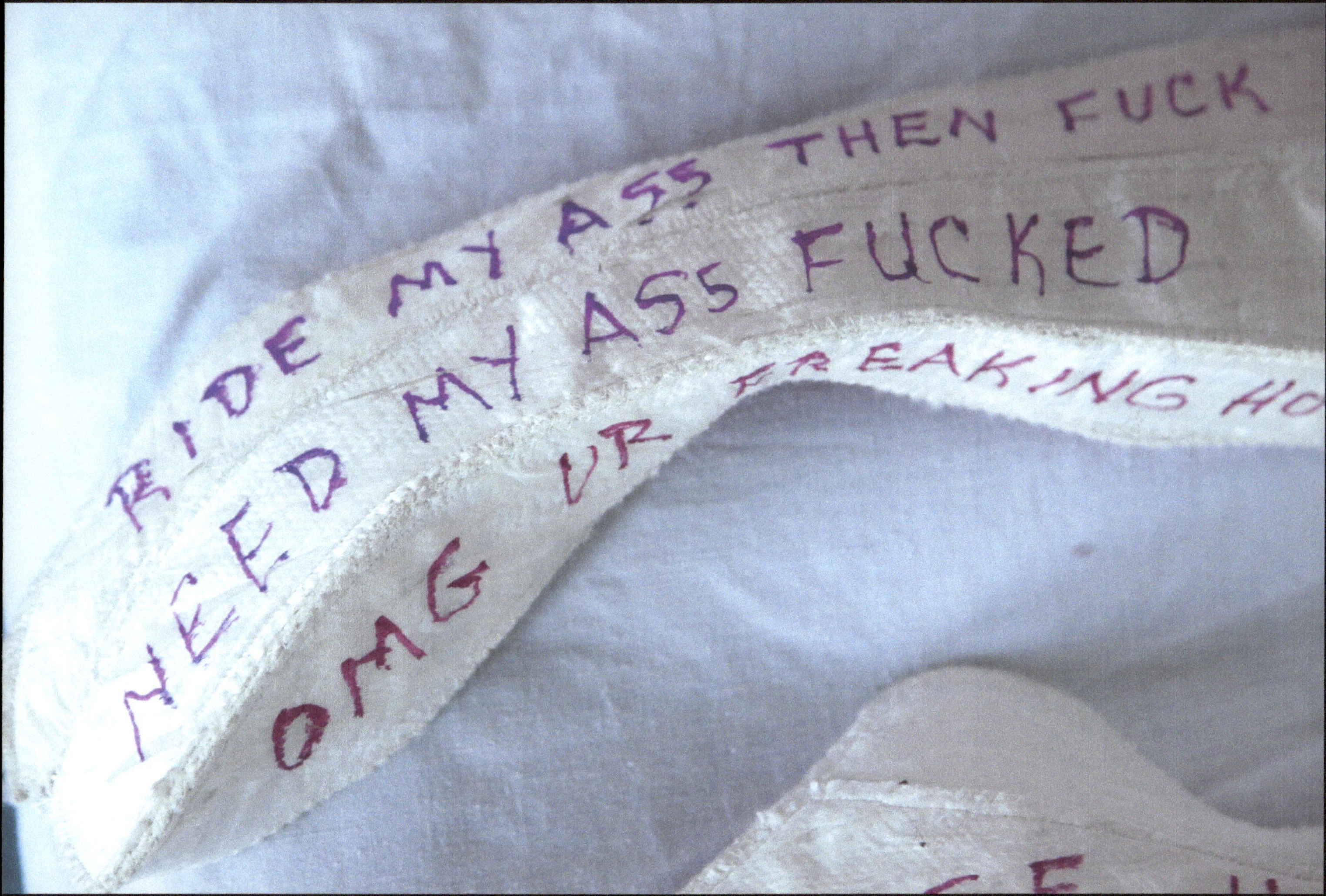
RIDE MY ASS THEN FUCK
NEED MY ASS FUCKED
OMG UR FREAKING HO

This project began when I thought about women, power, and powerlessness. As I researched domestic violence and prostitution, I discovered how young the women are on the street.

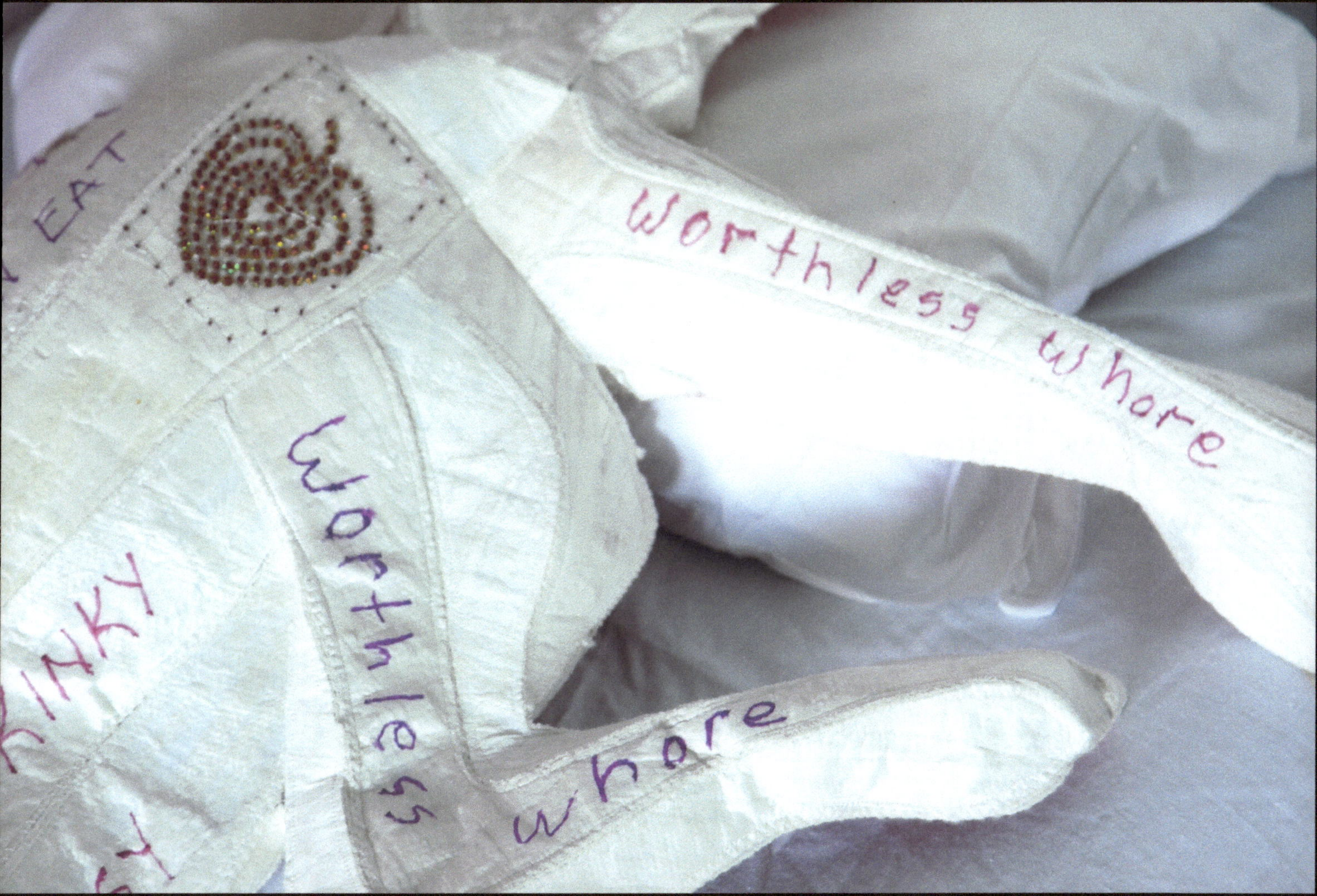
EAT
worthless whore
worthless
whore

One girl stated: "It's the only form of child abuse where the victim goes to jail.

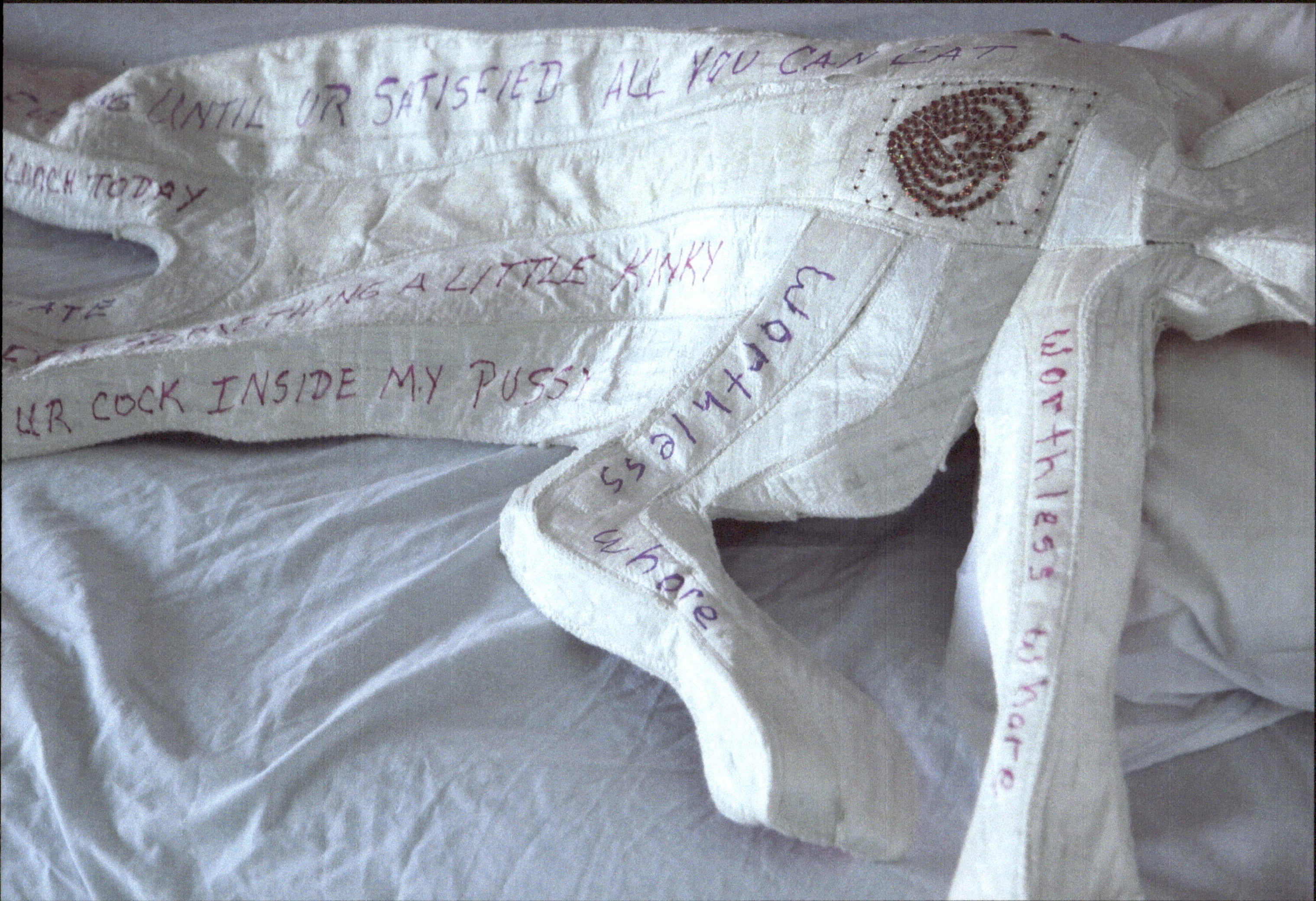
UNTIL UR SATISFIED ALL YOU CAN
TODAY
A LITTLE KINKY
UR COCK INSIDE MY
worthless whore
worthless whore

Research indicates that internet pornography has increased the violence against women. After all, "they" are just things, bought and paid for. A man can do what he wants to her, even if it almost kills her.

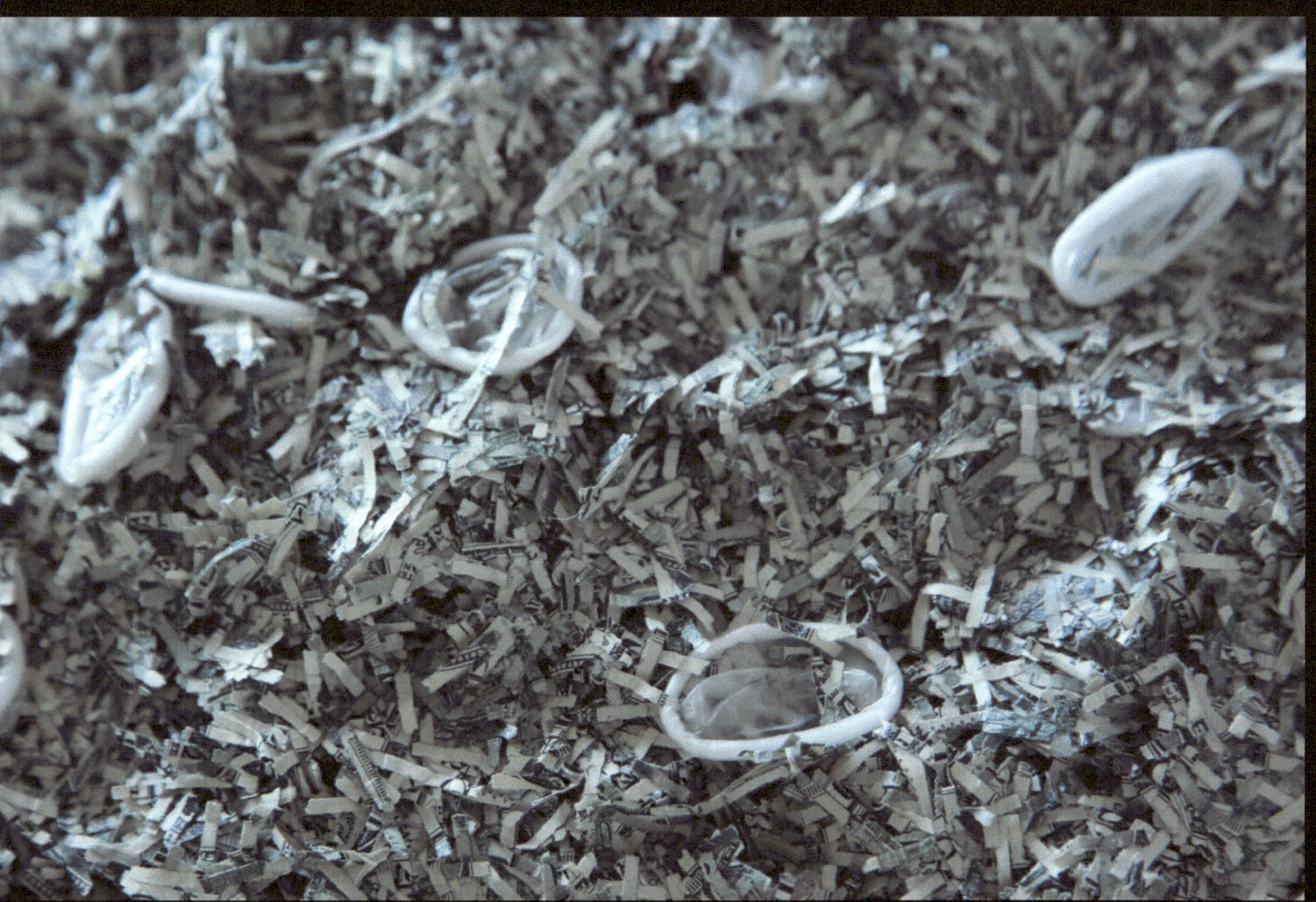

In my research, I came across a statement that said Americans have a great deal of sympathy for the foreign nationals that are trafficked into our country, but if they see an American girl on the street, they wonder: "Why did she choose this lifestyle?"

Average of young woman on the street is 14

Average of young woman on the street is 14

a prostitute in 10 days

any woman can be turned into a prostitute in

Too often the young women are runaways, some from incest, some from foster care so bad that the streets look better than where they are living.

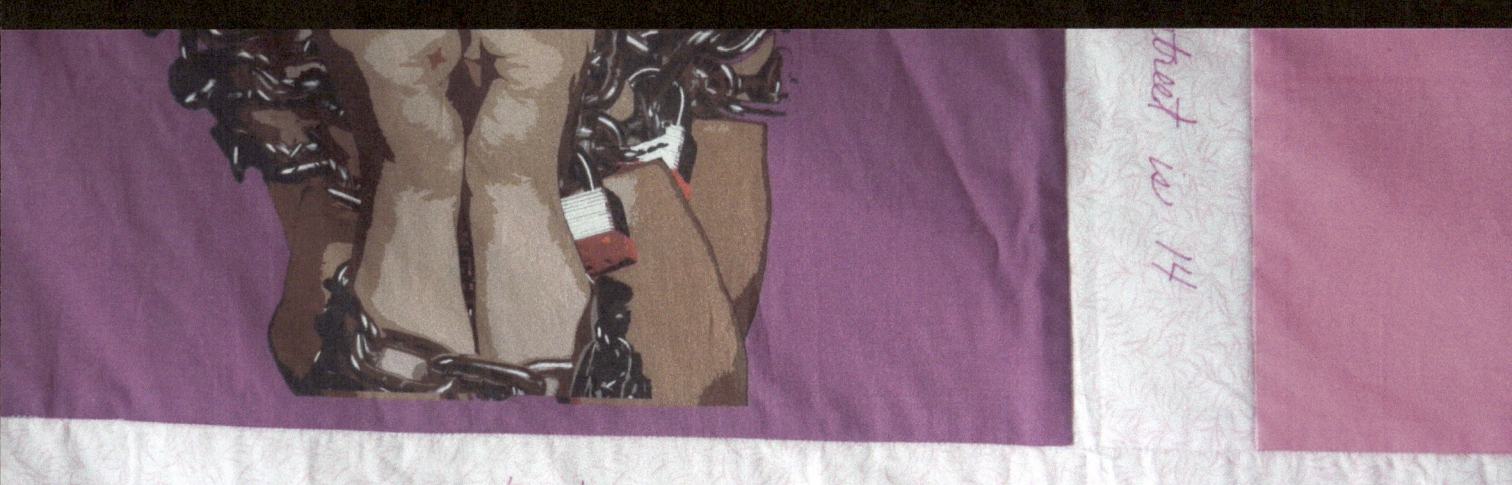

any woman can be turned into a prostitute in 10 days

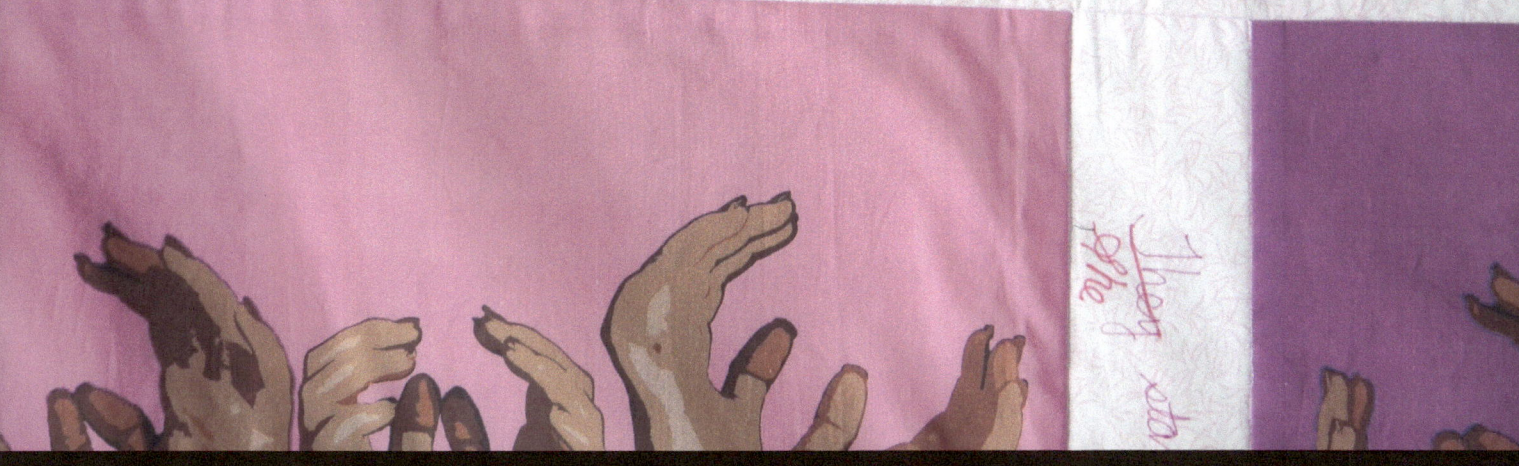

We have failed these young women in every way that counts.

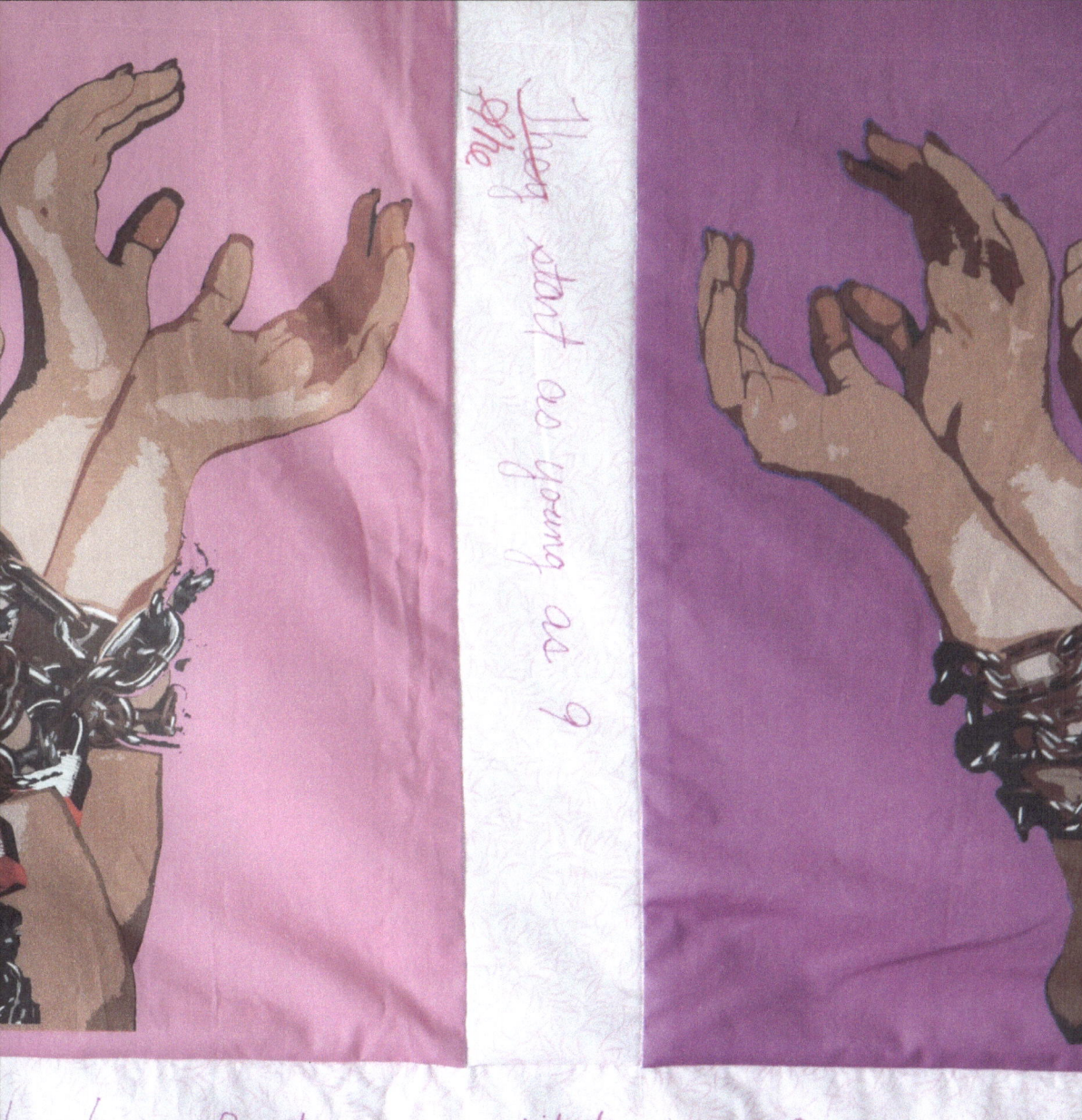

They start as young as 9 she be turned into a prostitute in 10 days

In a TakeAction.feeIdentity.com video regarding the sex slave trade, the number one is mentioned. You can be that one person. Please give your money and time to an organization of your choice.

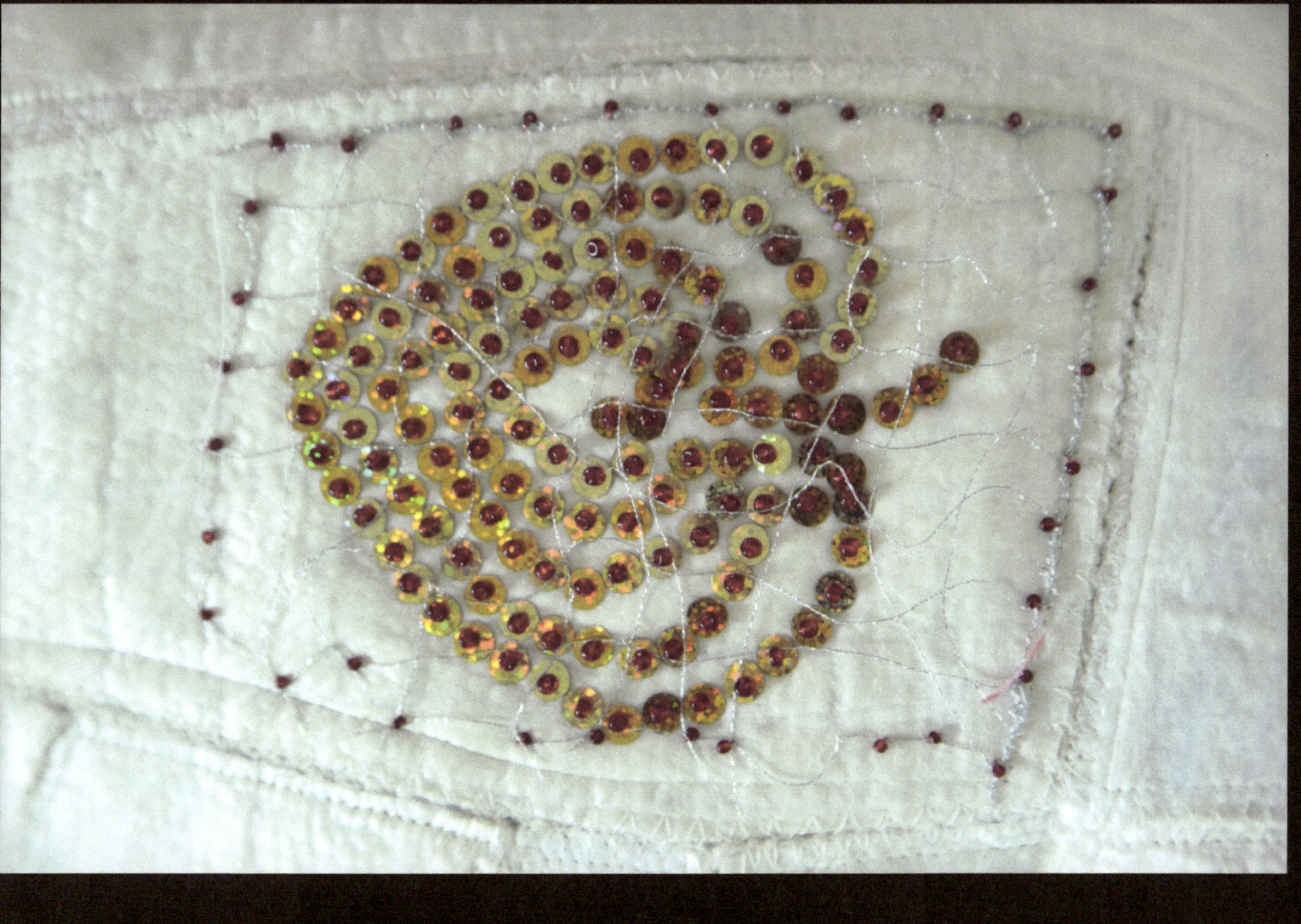

Debra Calkins

LongWalkHomeStudio.com

Debra@LongWalkHomeStudio.com

Stephanie Patrick, Singer, Songwriter

Michael Stadler, Photographer

StadlerStudio.com

Mail@StadlerStudio.com

REFERENCE

WalkingFree.org

PolarisProject.org

US Dept of Health & Human Services

US Dept of State

United Nations

UNICEF

OutofDarkness.org

TakeAction.TeenIdentity.com

Dr. Richard Poulin, University of Montreal. "Legalizing Prostitution
        Increases Human Trafficking"

Human Trafficking, Christina Fisanick, book editor

Human Trafficking Around the World   Kaye Stearman

CraigsList